BLENHEIM PALACE

GW00675946

BLENHEIM PALACE, home of the 11th Duke of Marlborough and birthplace of Sir Winston Churchill was built for John Churchill, 1st Duke of Marlborough, by Sir John Vanbrugh between the years 1705 and 1722.

The land and a sum of £240,000 were given to the Duke by a munificent sovereign, Queen Anne, and a grateful nation in recognition of his great victory over the French and Bavarians at the Battle of Blenheim 1704.

Apart from Vanbrugh, who designed the Palace in the Baroque style, other famous architects, craftsmen and landscape gardeners have been involved in the construction and development of Blenheim. The original gardens were designed by Queen Anne's gardener Henry Wise with later (1760s) alterations by Lancelot 'Capability' Brown which included the creation of Blenheim's most outstanding feature, the lake. In more recent times the French architect, Achille Duchêne, built the formal gardens to the east and west of the Palace. Hawksmoor, Grinling Gibbons, Yenn and Chambers also contributed to the Palace and gardens as we see them today.

The Estate consists of some 11,000 acres including the Park (2,100 acres) which is surrounded by a 9 mile long dry stone wall. The land usages are farming, both in hand and tenanted, forestry (including a sawmill and timber yard) and amenity. The Palace, Park and Gardens are open to the public and have been since Easter Sunday 1950. Whilst a continuous programme of development of facilities for visitors takes place, the overriding factor is that whatever is planned is in keeping, for example The Marlborough Maze. Of vital importance are the conservation, restoration and preservation of the Palace and Park as a unique and important part of Britain's National Heritage, for the benefit of generations to come.

VIEWS OF BLENHEIM.

This series of beautiful and fascinating pictures will, we hope, illustrate some of the many facets of Blenheim mentioned earlier. We hope you will enjoy them and that they will either remind you of your time here, or inspire you to visit. You will be most welcome.

The East Front and Italian Garden in spring.

The East Gate with the East Court and Clock Tower. The gates themselves weigh 17 tons and were shown at the Great Exhibition of 1851.

The Upper Terraces of the Water Gardens, design by the French architect Achille Duchêne under the guidance of the 9th Duke. Built 1925-30.

The Great Hall. 70 feet long, 40 feet wide and 67 feet high this remarkable room truly is great. Dominated by Vanbrugh's proscenium arch, embellished with the arms of Queen Anne, and with Thornhill's superb allegorical painting above, the Great Hall is a dramatic introduction to the splendours of Blenheim.

Opposite The China Ante Room. Blenheim's best know porcelain is displayed here—a Meissen dinner service of particular merit and interest. The King of Poland, in the mid 18th century, enquired from whom he could obtain a good pack of hounds and was told the Duke of Marlborough. The dogs were sent as a gift so the Duke was most surprised to be informed that a packing case, containing this service, and a bill of lading for £4, were at Tilbury Docks awaiting collection.

The Green Drawing Room. Over the fireplace hangs a full length portrait, by Romney, of George Spencer 4th Duke of Marlborough. It is fitting that in this room, which marks the beginning of the Palace tour, the man who made Blenheim, virtually, as it is seen today should take pride of place.

The Red Drawing Room. In which are two very important paintings. On the east wall Sir Joshua Reynolds' masterpiece the 4th Duke and family and opposite, John Singer Sergeants' study of the 9th Duke and family. Both paintings are of international renown and were recently exhibited in Washington (Treasure Houses of Great Britain Exhibition) and London (The Reynolds Exhibition).

The East Front from the Italian Garden. The wing including the famous Bow Window room, beneath which the foundation stone of Blenheim was laid, it was designed as and still is the private apartments of the Palace.

The South Front from the South West.

The North Front from the North West. The dappled sunlight and shadows emphasise Vanbrugh's fantastic roof line.

The upper terrace of the water gardens and West Front. The West Wing, over 190 feet in length houses the Long Library containing 10,000 volumes.

The Saloon or State Dining Room. At Christmas the Duke and his family dine here. The pollard oak dining table extends to over 25 feet enabling up to forty places to be set.

Dean Jones' Room. Dean Jones was the 1st Duke's Chaplain and was said to haunt this room. On 30th November 1874 Sir Winston Churchill was born here and the ghost has not been seen since that day!

The Long Library. Over 183 feet in length, was built as the Palace's picture gallery. At one time Van Dyck's huge equestrian portrait of Charles I hung at the northern end (this painting is now in the National Gallery). It is sometimes used for concerts and recitals when the wonderful sound of the magnificent Willis organ echoes throughout the Palace.

The 'Blenheim' tapestry, Green Writing Room. Blenheim's greatest treasure is the most famous panel of 'The Marlborough Victories' and was woven in the workshops of Judocus De Vos. Marlborough is seen receiving the surrender of Marshall Tallard. To the left is the village of Blindheim, from which the Palace took its name.

The First State Room. The Italian cradle was a gift to Consuelo, 9th Duchess, from her mother. It is a copy of one in the Doges Palace Venice, and used for the 10th Duke and his brother Lord Ivor Spencer Churchill.

The First State Room. The superb craftsmanship of the cabinet makers, imported from Paris by the 9th Duke, is highlighted in the overdoors which are copies of the boiseries of Louis XIV's bedroom in Versailles.

Queen Anne by Michael Rysbrack, (the Long Library) Commissioned by Sarah, 1st Duchess, in 1735 this fine statue once stood in the Library's bow window. It was moved in 1889 when the installation of the Willis organ began.

The Grand Entrance Doors and Lock. Said to be a copy of the city gates lock of Warsaw - no documentation exists - this magnificent example of British craftsmanship (it was made in Birmingham) is unique. It is complemented by its 'Coronet' key weighing $3\frac{1}{2}$lbs.

The chapel is still used by the family especially at Christmas when, joined by Estate staff and their families, Holy Communion is celebrated. The family vaults are under the chapel and Rysbracks massive memorial is a fitting reminder of the Great Duke's triumphs.

The Lower Water Terrace in autumn. The huge terracotta urn's displays which
are altered according to season, harmonise with the autumn gold of the trees.
And, throughout Blenheim's Gardens and Park, an abundance of rich hues of red,
gold and yellow continue the theme.

The Great Court showing two faces of the East Court. The wrought iron gates were installed by the 9th Duke during restoration.

The West, or unfinished, Court. Although perfect symmetry was intended to prevail at Blenheim in Vanburgh's original plan, economic necessity won the day. The stable block tower has only an outline of a clock and the courtyard was never completed.

The South Front in summer from the South East. On a summer afternoon the
welcome shade of a Copper Beach brings cool relief from the sun's rays. The Palace
glows yellow in the strong sunlight and is strangely quiet.

Vanbrugh's distinctive towers and gilded copper follies form the upper framework of a delightful scene.

'The Blenheim International Horse Trials'. Few sporting events can have a backdrop of such beauty, in the foreground two riders put their mounts through practice runs in the dressage arena.

The Vintage Car Club of Great Britain's sixteen finalists in the Great Court, complementing Vanbrugh's imposing portico. Rolls, Royce and Vanbrugh - what a combination of British genius?

The Column of Victory. Begun five years after Marlborough's death it is 134 feet high including the fine lead statue of the Duke, by Robert Pit, which surmounts it. Visitors should try to make time to walk up the hill to read the panegyric (inscription) — written by Lord Bolingbroke, (ironically the plotter of Marlborough's downfall.)

Queen Pool, Elizabeth Island and Palace. This viewpoint is near the Fisheries Cottage and well worth the walk. An additional delight is the noisy congregation of waterfowl that gather here in the shallow water to steal, or share, the food of the domestic hens.

The Lake from The Grand Bridge. Although the Palace is closed in the winter a visit to the Park is a visually rewarding experience. Views, such as this one are delightful ... and the exercise most beneficial!

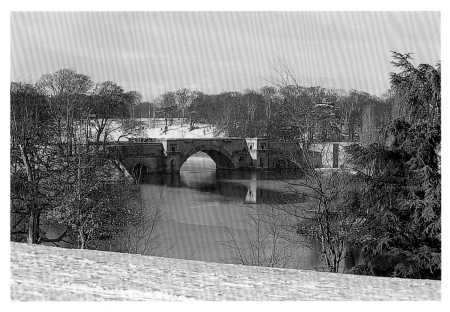

The Grand Bridge. Snow, ice, bare trees and pale winter sunshine cannot diminish the splendour of Vanbrugh's masterly design.

The 1st Duke and family by Closterman.

Consuelo, 9th Duchess by Carolus Duran, the first State Room.

The ceiling of the Great Hall painted by Sir James Thornhill. Marlborough is seen presenting the plan of the Battle of Blenheim to Britannia.

The West Front in winter from the Lower Water Terrace. Unless there is unseasonable snow in Spring, this view is one visitors may only see in a photograph, as the Palace is closed in the winter months.

However, the camera has captured the magic of the scene. The frozen ponds and pristine snow, etch in sharpest detail, the fantastic roof line of the Palace against the clear blue winter sky.

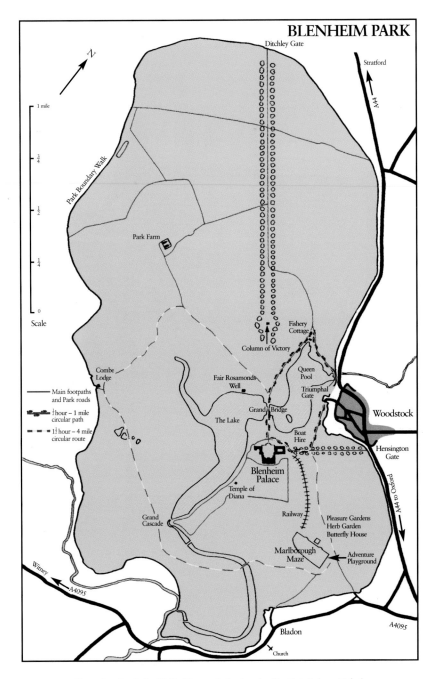

BLENHEIM PARK

Ditchley Gate

Stratford

A44

Park Boundary Walk

Park Farm

Fishery Cottage

Column of Victory

Combe Lodge

Fair Rosamonds Well

Queen Pool

Triumphal Gate

Grand Bridge

The Lake

Boat Hire

Woodstock

Hensington Gate

Blenheim Palace

Temple of Diana

Railway

A44 to Oxford

Grand Cascade

Pleasure Gardens
Herb Garden
Butterfly House

Witney

A4095

Marlborough Maze

Adventure Playground

Bladon

Church

A4095

1 mile

¾

½

¼

0

Scale

N

Main footpaths and Park roads

½ hour – 1 mile circular path

1½ hour – 4 mile circular route

Text and captions by Paul Duffie. Photographed and produced by Chris Andrews, Oxford